The Pet Rap

By Sally Cowan

I am Reb.

I can rap, rap, rap!

Rib sits at my hip.

Rib fits in my cap!

Tam has a pet.

Her pet is Pip.

Tim has Mits.

Sit, sit, sit!

I am Reb

and Rib fits in my cap.

CHECKING FOR MEANING

1. Who is the main character in the story? *(Literal)*

2. What kind of pet does Reb have? *(Literal)*

3. Why do you think Reb enjoys rapping about pets? *(Inferential)*

EXTENDING VOCABULARY

rap	Look at the word *rap*. How many sounds are in the word? What are other words you can think of that rhyme with *rap*?
fits	What does it mean if Rib *fits* in Reb's cap? What other animals could fit in a cap?
cap	A *cap* is worn on your head. What other words describe things you can wear on your head?

MOVING BEYOND THE TEXT

1. Why is a rat a good pet?

2. Why do you think Reb wrote a rap about pets?

3. Who might like to hear Reb's rap? Why?

4. What would you like to write a rap about? Why?

SPEED SOUNDS

| Cc | Bb | Rr | Ee | Ff | Hh | Nn |
| Mm | Ss | Aa | Pp | Ii | Tt |

PRACTICE WORDS

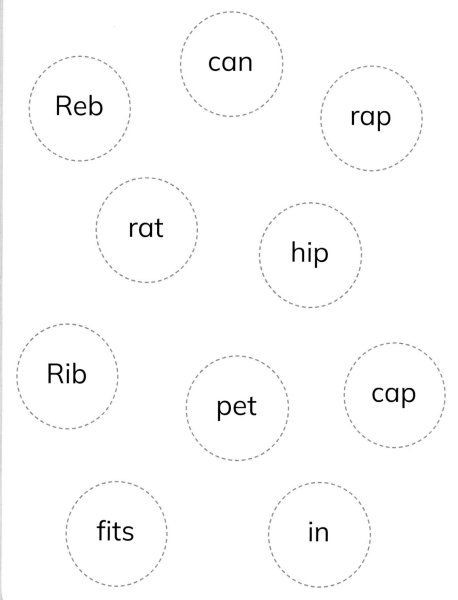

can

Reb

rap

rat

hip

Rib

pet

cap

fits

in